2 Minute EFT Meridian Tapping Routines for Wealth Health Love Happiness and more, se!*

Introduction...page 3

Chapter 1: Receiving Massive Abundance...page 8

Chapter 2: I Don't Procrastinate, I Take Action...page 10

Chapter 3: Eating Healthy and Resisting Food Cravings...page 12

Chapter 4: Being Jovial and Living Happy...page 13

Chapter 5: Enjoying Money...page 14

Chapter 6: My Laser-sharp Focus keeps me on the Path...page 15

Chapter 7: Checking my Baggage and Re-inventing Myself...page 16

Chapter 8: I Love and am Grateful for My Body...page 17

Chapter 9: My Life is an Easy Celebration!...page 18

Chapter 10: Love flows into me and I Radiate Love out...page 19

Chapter 11: I Control my Emotions and Maintain Serenity...page 20

Chapter 12: I Am Appreciated, Successful and Wealthy...page 21

Chapter 13: I can Live a Joyful Life even with Physical Discomfort...page 23

Chapter 14: I Love myself too much to allow myself to Live in Fear...page 24

Chapter 15: Done with Self-Sabotage, Moving on to Self-Esteem...page 26

Chapter 16: I Am Vibrantly Alive and can choose to Live a long Life...page 28

Chapter 17: I Choose Ease, Peace and Serenity instead of Depression...page 30

Chapter 18: I Am Ready to Receive my Soulmate now!...page 32

Chapter 19: Moving closer to Joy and Myself by Identifying and pursuing my Life's Purpose(s)...page 34

Chapter 20: I attract as many Lovers as I wish to have...page 36

Chapter 21: Your Customizable Template...page 38

Introduction

Hello and welcome! This little book contains easy-to-use tools that can transform your entire life! Meridian tapping is a powerful technique that is the result of both ancient Eastern knowledge and modern knowledge. Modern science has confirmed that the energy meridian lines mapped out by Taoists, and others, thousands of years ago correspond to actual physiological structures in our body. Meridian tapping pairs our specific thoughts with our body's energy system, and we are then able to shift our beliefs by moving our body's energies. By tapping on our actual energy meridians we can clear energetic blockages, which then helps unblock mental or emotional blockages. Another way of describing it is by changing the way we FEEL we change the way we THINK which changes our BELIEFS which changes our ACTIONS which changes our lives. Try it out for a "test drive" and see if you can notice a difference in yourself!

The routines in this book are designed to eliminate negative beliefs, release emotional blockages, increase the amount of joy in your life, increase your wealth and flow of abundance, increase the amount of love in your life, and get you back in dialogue (and love) with your body and your true, powerful self. I realize that some of the statements in the routines may sound a little flowery or optimistic to some, but I have actually come to see the statements listed here as truths in my personal life. Just a few years ago I would never have believed that life could almost always be fun and easy, but now my life really is like that!

To perform tapping, begin by bending your little finger and ring finger down and holding them with your thumb while keeping your middle and index fingers up and together (see Figure A). You can use either your right or left hand and tap on either side of your body.

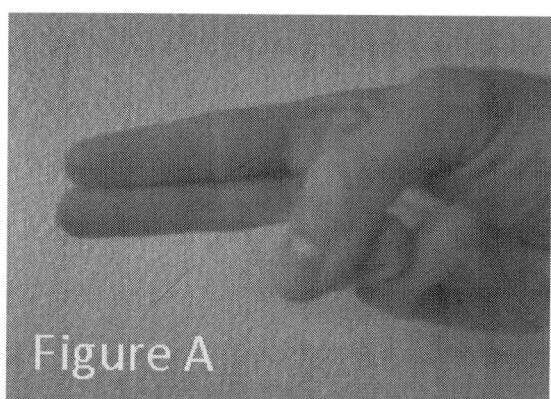

Figure A

To "tap" you simply strike the various tapping points on your body, one at a time, with the pads (skin on the other side from your fingernails) of your middle and index fingers at least seven times at each point (and then the process is usually repeated at least one more time). Don't tap too lightly, but never cause yourself any pain or discomfort.

We're going to use eight different tapping points beginning with the point just inside the beginning of your eyebrow (see Figure B).

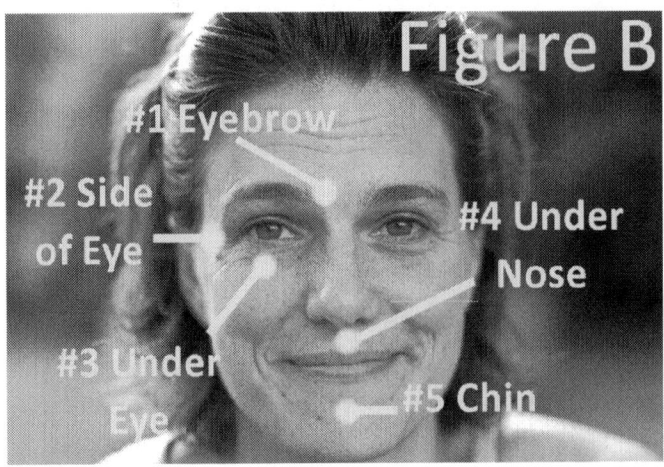

So get your fingers together as shown in Figure A and begin tapping point #1 near the start of one of your eyebrows while saying (out loud if possible), "In the past I have allowed myself to be ruled by fears which seemed to be real and powerful." Then move on to tapping point #2 on the side of your eye (see Figure B) and tap there while saying "I have also allowed my Now to be less joyful because I was busy worrying about something that might happen in the future." Then move on to tapping point #3 below your eye (see Figure B) and tap there while saying "Many people live nearly all of their lives in the shadow of fear." Then move on to tapping point #4 below your nose (see Figure B) and tap there while saying "Some people refuse to experience fear and never remain in extended periods of being fearful." Then move on to tapping point #5 on your chin (see Figure B) and tap there while saying "I am someone who is choosing not to tolerate fear in my life."

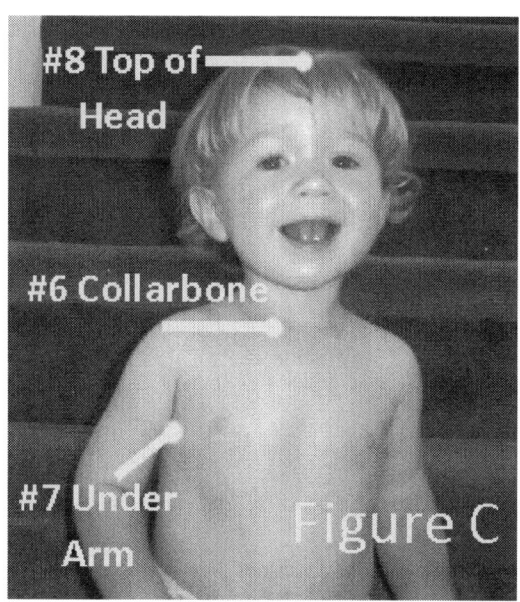

Then move on to tapping point #6 on the lower part of your collarbone (see Figure C) and tap there while saying "I will never again believe that the world is inherently difficult, dangerous or uncaring." Then move on to tapping point #7 underneath your arm [you'll have to raise your arm up a little] (see Figure C) and tap there while saying "The Universe could have made another galaxy in a second, but instead it chose to make me." [Throughout this book, instead of using the phrase "The Universe" you can say "God", "Providence", "Source" or whatever word or phrase you would like to use.] Then move on to tapping point #8 on the top, center of your head (see Figure C) and tap there while saying "I am part of existence and I am an important, loved child of the Universe."

Now we are going to continue this tapping routine by tapping on the 8 points again while saying these phrases...

Eyebrow: I don't fear the world because it is merely another creation of the same force that created me

Side of eye: While it's true that other people fear, I have chosen not to be like them

Under eye: In the past I have adopted other people's fears because I am a very sensitive, aware person

Under nose: I even used to accept other people's fears just to be liked and not stand out

Chin: But now I CHOSE to stand out as one of those amazing people who don't live in fear

Collarbone: If someone wants to, or can't help but, judge me or dislike me for not fearing then I will simply gift them with my company less often

Under arm: I have the right to enjoy my life!

Top of Head: Instead of listening to my non-productive, monkey-mind chatter I'm going to smile at myself in the mirror and tell myself that I'm cute!

Just for good measure, let's continue this energetic/mind clearing by tapping on the 8 points again while saying the phrase listed next to each point. [Most of the clearing routines in this book only cycle through the 8 tapping points twice.]

Eyebrow: People worry about money when really all money is is a reflection of how much personal power one allows oneself to wield

Side of eye: Other people worry about things because they are resistant to life or are out of touch with who they really are

Under eye: I consistently choose peace over drama. I can embrace even "bad" news and make it lose its power.

Under nose: I win by remaining in a state of allowance

Chin: I remain in a state of Faith; Faith in myself and faith in my response to anything outside of myself.

Collarbone: When I live in a state of fearless Faith I can see opportunities and beautiful possibilities that people who live in fear cannot see

Under arm: The degree to which I stop fearing and allow myself to have an abundant life of ease is the degree to which I love myself

Top of head: I am stepping out from the dark shadow of fear and am now someone who refuses to fear anything!

Now... ask yourself if you feel somewhat relieved and relaxed. :o)

The next thing to do is check out the table of contents and zoom to the chapters that address issues that you are facing in order to help respond to them in an enlightened manner. Feel free to write the routines out on paper and/or modify them in order to precisely match your specific needs and beliefs. You should do the tapping routine twice a day for as long as you feel you need to; you can do the same routine every day forever if you wish. Leave yourself a little sticky-note reminder, or some digital reminder, to remind yourself to do your daily tapping! Have fun with it!

Chapter 1: Receiving Massive Abundance

I am the wise person who can receive massive abundance effortlessly!

Eyebrow: In the past I have had a problem with receiving

Side of eye: That's why I had been living in survival mode

Under eye: I used to think that money meant a lot of hard work so I rejected it

Under nose: I used to think that money is for people who have misplaced priorities

Chin: ...or are too busy to enjoy life

Collarbone: I didn't used to even think of myself as the kind of person who could have a lot of money

Under arm: ...because I value freedom and I value time to do what I want to do

Top of head: But now I have decided that I am ready to receive effortlessly

Eyebrow: I know now that it doesn't take a lot of hard work to receive a lot of money

Side of eye: Money is a sign of appreciation that people exchange for something they value

Under eye: I can make a lot of money just by listening to my heart, doing what I like, and giving other people things they value!

Under nose: I can visualize myself as a wealthy person who does what I want to do when I want to do it

Chin: Having a lot of money helps me to have more freedom and more free time

Collarbone: I like the FEELING of being wealthy, and the more I stay in that feeling the more wealth is attracted to me ... as if by magic!

Under arm: Now I can show other people how easy it is to receive sooo much

Top of head: Now that I have allowed myself to receive wealth I can see myself as an inspiration to others and I am more generous than ever!

Chapter 2: I Don't Procrastinate, I Take Action

I will stop Procrastinating and no longer put my Dreams on hold

Eyebrow: In the past I would often wait until the last minute to do things

Side of eye: I would often complete work or projects right before the deadline as a way to "get back" at the person who assigned the work to me

Under eye: But often I procrastinate doing things that I want to do

Under nose: I often don't do things that are really important to me because I don't feel as though the time is right

Chin: ...or I think that I'm not ready yet

Collarbone: ...or because I fear failing or being "rejected"

Under arm: What if I could operate without fear?

Top of head: I want to move confidently in the direction of my dreams

Eyebrow: I'm ready to actually achieve that which I know is possible

Side of eye: I'm going to stop getting in the way of my greatness

Under eye: Even when it's something that someone else wants me to do I can either say "no" to them or choose to serve them graciously

Under nose: I'm going to write out my dreams, figure out what is the first step towards actualizing them, and take action

Chin: The only failure is not trying. The only people who don't make mistakes are those that aren't learning or doing anything new

Collarbone: I'm going to be true to myself, start living my dreams, focus on what gets me started, and not give any energy to anything that slows me down

Under arm: I don't need to see the entire path to get there, often it isn't until after I take the first step towards my ideal reality that the next step is revealed to me

Top of head: I am able to move forward virtually effortlessly, and making progress makes me so happy!

Chapter 3: Eating Healthy and Resisting Food Cravings

Eyebrow: I know that the quality of food I eat affects both my body and mind

Side of eye: I enjoy having energy, thinking clearly and being vibrantly healthy

Under eye: As a child of the Universe I deserve to have the best foods nature offers

Under nose: I'm not going to eat much cheap, processed food anymore

Chin: I deserve better than that!

Collarbone: When I shop for food I buy whole foods in their natural state

Under arm: I don't buy foods full of chemicals, preservatives, or fruit or vegetables that are sprayed with pesticides

Top of head: I know that if I only have good, healthy food around I will eat a lot of good, healthy food!

Eyebrow: I will plan out my meals

Side of eye: ...so that even when I'm on the go I will have healthy foods to eat

Under eye: I can see myself carrying apples and bananas instead of soda or candy

Under nose: I will buy special, clean water to drink at home and take some with me in a nice container when I go out

Chin: When I have a craving for an unhealthy food I laugh and feel good knowing that I am no longer a slave to foods like that

Collarbone: I know that people who have been eating healthy for several months seldom crave foods that are not good for their bodies

Under arm: I can sooo be one of those people!

Top of head: I am choosing NOW to be one of those people!

Chapter 4: Being Jovial and Living Happy

Moving from Being Serious most of the time to Being Seriously Jovial

Eyebrow: In my past I was worrying and stressing about stuff too much

Side of eye: I look back on parts of my life and I wish I had allowed myself to make the best of my situation and enjoy life more back then

Under eye: But I can't go back and change the past

Under nose: But I can absolutely decide what I want my now and my future to be like!

Chin: I can decide to spend less time worrying and more time focusing on things that delight me

Collarbone: By just continually focusing on following my bliss NOW

Under arm: ...I am ensuring that my future will be as full of fun and happiness as it can be!

Top of head: I am raising my silliness setpoint!

Eyebrow: I'm done worrying about stuff

Side of eye: I'm shifting from fear to faith

Under eye: Worrying is useless and I want to have fun!

Under nose: I choose fun!

Chin: I choose happiness!

Collarbone: I'm not going to let unhappy people drag me down to their level

Under arm: I will move towards the sound of laughter

Top of head: ...and those that love to laugh will move towards me!

Chapter 5: Enjoying Money

Money is fun!

Eyebrow: Here's that money issue

Side of eye: It's kind of scary

Under eye: I don't know if I even want to think about it

Under nose: I was told money was the root of all evil

Chin: ...and I think that some people do bad things to get money

Collarbone: I don't even like to ask for things

Under arm: ...or use up all my favors with the Universe

Top of head: But money is fun to have

Eyebrow: Money relieves my stress

Side of eye: I know that there is more money in the world now than there ever has been before

Under eye: The perceived LACK of money is the root of all evil

Under nose: ...and the Universe that created me wants me to enjoy great abundance in all good, fun things

Chin: ...because It loves me and knows that I will use money to do beneficial things

Collarbone: I'm ready to receive money and have a fun relationship with sexy money

Under arm: The more money I have the more generous and helpful I can be

Top of Head: Universe, please give me more money than I can even spend!

Chapter 6: My Laser-sharp Focus keeps me on the Path

Eyebrow: In the past I have been scatter-brained and unfocused at times

Side of eye: But now I'm making a choice to keep my mind focused

Under eye: Life with my new calm, focused mind is far easier than my life was back when my mind would race around

Under nose: ... burning itself out trying to figure everything out or worrying about every little thing

Chin: I no longer have to judge or analyze everything

Collarbone: I can just ask myself, "Does this bring me closer to what I want?"

Under arm: "Does this bring me closer to the energies I want to embrace?"

Top of head: "Does this bring me closer to ME?!"

Eyebrow: I focus on what I want and I am pulled toward it through my intention

Side of eye: All I have to do is think about what I like, love and want!

Under eye: I don't have to get mired down in all the things the collective [un]consciousness wastes its time brooding about

Under nose: I know what I want and I'm getting it!

Chin: Many people in this world are busy being frantic

Collarbone: ...but while they are all distracted I have secretly given myself a promotion

Under arm: I can just relax my body, head, face and gut, knowing that I am moving towards where I want to go

Top of head: I follow my bliss and enjoy moving forward into the wonderful future I envision for myself

Chapter 7: Checking my Baggage and Re-inventing Myself

I'm leaving all my Old Baggage behind and moving into a wonderful Future

Eyebrow: There have been times in my life when I have been emotionally injured by people or events

Side of eye: ...but I'm not going to define myself by my reactions to those events

Under eye: I am a dynamic, ever-changing person

Under nose: I may even be an eternal being

Chin: If I hold on to the past I have no future and am limiting myself so much!

Collarbone: I am going to forgive myself for anything I think I did wrong

Under arm: I am going to forgive others for anything I think they did wrong

Top of head: ahhh... forgiving others is a gift to myself!

Eyebrow: I don't ever need to worry about making a mistake again

Side of eye: ...because I know that I like myself enough to forgive myself

Under eye: I can go forward *expecting* to be delighted

Under nose: I'm going to put the past way behind me so all I can see in front of me is my clear, bright future

Chin: Every day I can decide what adventures I wish to have and re-invent myself. Every day is a good day. Every day is a play day!

Collarbone: I can be as giddy and full of energy as a playful, curious kid and give myself permission to do whatever I want to do each day

Under arm: I enjoy my now and visualize what my delightful future will look like

Top of head: Freedom and joy. I'm feeling it. I'm being it. I'm living it!

Chapter 8: I Love and am Grateful for My Body

Eyebrow: In the past certain aspects of my body have made me sad

Side of eye: I had judged my body and decided that parts of it didn't look or operate right

Under eye: ...but my body has gotten me this far

Under nose: ...and my body needs someone to love it

Chin: If I love my body will it glow like the body of someone in love?

Collarbone: I can accept my body and love it just the way it is

Under arm: I will open a dialogue with my body

Top of head: My body can tell me how to help it look and feel better

Eyebrow: I can improve my body by cleansing my mind and body of toxic thoughts and substances

Side of eye: My body glows when I am true to myself and stay in the vibrations of positive thoughts and energies

Under eye: I can eat more fruits and vegetables, do breath work, and move my body in any way that feels good.

Under nose: I clear any energy or feelings of judgment, insecurity, doubt, worry, fear or lack from my body

Chin: I run my hands over my body and say "I care"

Collarbone: Every one of the 72 trillion cells in my body will vibrate at the energy of love, peace, gratitude and joy

Under arm: I feel magnificent!

Top of head: I love my body... thank you body!

Chapter 9: My Life is an Easy Celebration!

I will never stay Stressed or Anxious again!

Eyebrow: I've noticed that in the past I've been tense and stressed out at times

Side of eye: I had conditioned myself to fall into a default state of worry

Under eye: I had conditioned myself to find things to worry about

Under nose: ...but I can decide to take charge of my mind

Chin: I am the President and Chief Executive Officer of my mind!

Collarbone: I will make ease, joy and lightness my priorities

Under arm: I will relax my entire face, head and body. I can do whatever I want or need to do, but I will be relaxed while doing it.

Top of head: I can choose to smile, laugh and see everything in a humorous light, and no one can stop me!

Eyebrow: I can avoid traffic stress by leaving early

Side of eye: I can avoid lunchtime stress by packing a healthy snack in my bag

Under eye: I can avoid accepting the stresses of anyone around me

Under nose: I can just place my hand over my heart and say to myself "I love you"

Chin: I can happily achieve or do nothing. Sometimes the more the effort, the more the ego.

Collarbone: I am going to abandon fear and choose faith

Under arm: I trust that this Universe I was born into has my back

Top of head: As President of my life, I now proclaim my life to be an easy celebration!

Chapter 10: Love flows into me and I Radiate Love out

Love and Caring from Above, please flow through me to Here

Eyebrow: I want to increase the amount of love in my life

Side of eye: I want love to flow into me

Under eye: I want love to flow out of me

Under nose: I want to be a conduit for the Universal energy of love to flow through

Chin: I may not understand the depth of this love at first

Collarbone: …but I am open to accepting this experience

Under arm: I am asking the Universe to help me live in a wide field of love

Top of head: I am surrounded by a deep, unconditional love

Eyebrow: I invite this amazing energy into my heart and body

Side of eye: I receive more love than my body can contain and naturally this love will spill over to everyone and everything around me

Under eye: People around me will feel how strong my love energies are

Under nose: I offer love even to people who are unwilling to accept my gift

Chin: …because I know that some day they will be able to understand how wonderful and valuable it is to be in the flow of love

Collarbone: Despite the skewed news reports, the world is absolutely becoming a more peaceful, loving place!

Under arm: I will help usher in a new age of Love in this physical dimension

Top of head: Our love not only can, but IS changing the world!

Chapter 11: I Control my Emotions and Maintain Serenity

Defusing annoyances, pet peeves and bad mood triggers

Eyebrow: There are some things in this world that I prefer not to hear, see or do

Side of eye: In the past I have allowed these things to affect my mood

Under eye: I have felt an opposition to these things in my mind

Under nose: I have felt an opposition to these things in my body

Chin: ...but I don't have to let my awareness of these feelings affect my mood

Collarbone: My happiness is something I control

Under arm: My happiness is not dependent on external circumstances

Top of head: I choose happy!

Eyebrow: Sometimes I think that I have to correct others

Side of eye: ...because their behavior seems unhelpful to me, themselves or others

Under eye: But if I know what they are doing

Under nose: ...then the Universe knows what they are doing

Chin: ...and the Universe will give them what they put out (Karma)

Collarbone: ...I don't need to say a word or lift a finger!

Under arm: I will practice not wearing my emotions on my sleeve

Top of head: ...so the next time I see a young spirit doing or saying something unenlightened I don't laugh or smile TOO much!

Chapter 12: I Am Appreciated, Successful and Wealthy

Eyebrow: Even though I have kept myself small in the past this has always been **my** choice, a decision I have made

Side of eye: I have allowed myself to experience struggle and financial hardship in order to have more in common with the majority of my brothers and sisters

Under eye: But now I realize that being wealthy is a choice, just as being happy is a choice, and I feel like being wealthy now

Under nose: I am ready to accept all the gifts that the Universe is offering me

Chin: I don't have to figure out exactly how other people will come to appreciate me

Collarbone: I am open to all of the infinite ways in which the Universe can lead me towards a serene, blissful life

Under arm: I am so grateful that I am able to have direct conversations with the Universe

Top of head: I am **ready** to receive my recognition and money now

Eyebrow: I am **willing** to receive my recognition and money now

Side of eye: I am **able** to receive my recognition and money now

Under eye: I can see my family and I living in an exquisite manner

Under nose: Everywhere I go I see joyful things and have wonderful things to do and think about

Chin: Life is pure pleasure and malls are fun

Collarbone: I feel valued, loved, appreciated, successful, wealthy and respected

Under arm: I am valued, loved, appreciated, successful, wealthy and respected

Top of Head: This vast Universe has enough abundance for everyone to succeed in life, have wealth, and enjoy their lives

Chapter 13: I can Live a Joyful Life even with Physical Discomfort

Eyebrow: My mind often tells me that there is something wrong with my body

Side of eye: It's a feeling of pain or discomfort in my body

Under eye: It's there to warn me of a danger there was to my body

Under nose: …like the pain of a burned finger teaches one not to touch a hot ring on a stove

Chin: But I got the message

Collarbone: …and I no longer need to hear the reminder

Under arm: I no longer need to feel the "pain alarm"

Top of head: I realize that my body is just trying to help me

Eyebrow: I am grateful for my body and all it has done for me

Side of eye: …and all it can still do for me

Under eye: Perhaps I will find a person who understands my body better than my doctor does who can disconnect my pain reminder

Under nose: In the meantime I can give love to my body

Chin: …and clear out any emotional, physical or energetic blockages it may have

Collarbone: I am so much more than my physical body

Under arm: I probably chose to have this challenge in this lifetime to prove just how far I have evolved and encourage myself to become even stronger

Top of head: The Universe only gives people what they can handle… I must be an amazingly strong soul!

Chapter 14: I Love myself too much to allow myself to Live in Fear

Eyebrow: In the past I have allowed myself to be ruled by fears which seemed to be real and powerful

Side of eye: I have also allowed my Now to be less joyful because I was busy worrying about something that might happen in the future

Under eye: Many people live nearly all of their lives in the shadow of fear

Under nose: Some people refuse to experience fear and never remain in extended periods of being fearful

Chin: I am someone who is choosing not to tolerate fear in my life

Collarbone: I will never again believe that the world is inherently difficult, dangerous or uncaring

Under arm: The Universe could have made another galaxy in a heartbeat, but instead it chose to make me

Top of head: I am part of existence and I am an important, loved child of the Universe

Eyebrow: I don't fear the world because it is merely another creation of the same force that created me

Side of eye: While it's true that other people fear, I have chosen not to be like them

Under eye: In the past I have adopted other people's fears because I am a very sensitive, aware person

Under nose: I even used to accept other people's fears just to be liked and not stick out

Chin: But now I CHOSE to stick out as one of those amazing people who don't live in fear

Collarbone: If someone wants to, or can't help but, judge me or dislike me for not fearing then I will simply gift them with my company less often

Under arm: I have the right to enjoy my life!

Top of Head: Instead of listening to my non-productive, monkey-mind chatter I'm going to smile at myself in the mirror and tell myself that I'm cute!

Eyebrow: People worry about money when really all money is is a reflection of the how much personal power one allows oneself to wield

Side of eye: Other people worry about things because they are resistant to life or are out of touch with who they really are

Under eye: I consistently choose peace over drama. I can embrace even "bad" news and make it lose its power.

Under nose: I win by remaining in a state of allowance

Chin: I remain in a state of Faith; Faith in myself and faith in my response to anything outside of myself.

Collarbone: When I live in a state of fearless Faith I can see opportunities and beautiful possibilities that people who live in fear cannot see

Under arm: The degree to which I stop fearing and allow abundance is the degree to which I love myself

Top of head: I am stepping out from the dark shadow of fear and am now someone who refuses to fear anything!

Chapter 15: Done with Self-Sabotage, Moving on to Self-Esteem

Eyebrow: In the past I have kept myself small

Side of eye: …I have been afraid to let myself be known

Under eye: …I have been afraid of making commitments to people or plans that could generate money or expand my life in new directions

Under nose: I understand that this was just my mind's attempt to keep me "safe"

Chin: I love that my mind always tries to keep me safe!

Collarbone: But I now realize that in the past I had actually been operating with such a deep-seated fear of the unknown that I kept myself smaller than I wish to be

Under arm: I am going to embrace change!

Top of head: I am going to become outwardly magnificent!

Eyebrow: I'm done confusing the feeling of EXCITEMENT with the feeling of FEAR

Side of eye: I'm going to bask in that strange, exciting feeling I get when I'm challenging myself and expanding!

Under eye: I am going to trust myself, receive more of ME and tap into my infinity

Under nose: I have no fears of being hurt, embarrassed or belittled because I love and respect myself too much to ever be ashamed of being me

Chin: I am going to take my leash off and allow myself to be successful with my wings fully spread

Collarbone: I'm not going to be alone if I become successful, I'll just have some new, wonderful, more dynamic friends in my life

Under arm: I'm ready to move into a higher realm of existence

Top of head: ...a reality where my exterior environment more closely matches my elevated levels of insight and self-respect

Chapter 16: I Am Vibrantly Alive and can choose to Live a long Life

"...as a geneticist, I'm really interested in epigenetic phenomenon, that is, the capacity of our genes to change in their expression as a function of experience. Meditation seems to do that as well."

- Dr. Susan Smalley

Eyebrow: I was raised to believe that my health will deteriorate as I get older

Side of eye: The media and medical industries tell us that we age

Under eye: I can see people around me looking older and even experiencing physical death

Under nose: I don't believe everything the companies doing business in the health care industry tell me

Chin: When I believe something the Universe shifts things around to support my belief

Collarbone: I believe that I'm much more than just predetermined DNA programming

Under arm: ...and my soul essence cannot actually age or die

Top of head: ...and those that I love have a life force in them that goes beyond this physical dimension

Eyebrow: I know that the media sometimes spins the facts, that's why I don't believe everything it says

Side of eye: I have heard of many reports of "spontaneous healing" and "miracles" in my lifetime

Under eye: I can affect my gene expression through my thoughts

Under nose: My cells can be nearly as infinite as my spiritual being

Chin: I will live as long as I wish, perhaps as long as the 200 year old Taoists lived

Collarbone: I choose to be completely healthy, and the people I love want to be healthy too

Under arm: The Universe is constantly offering me good food and encouraging me to move my body properly (for example, growing your own food gives you both exercise and healthy, fresh food)

Top of head: I love life and I will be a vibrantly alive part of the Physical Universe for as long as I choose to be!

Chapter 17: I Choose Ease, Peace and Serenity instead of Depression

Eyebrow: In the past I have let circumstances outside of myself affect my mood

Side of eye: I have let other people's worries cause me to worry

Under eye: …but I don't have to react like most people do

Under nose: I can have an enlightened response to any situation

Chin: I WILL have an enlightened response to any situation

Collarbone: I can remain calm no matter what is happening around me

Under arm: I make better decisions when I'm calm

Top of head: I can envision myself staying calm even when those around me are hysterical

Eyebrow: Other people may not understand how I am able to be calm and collected all the time

Side of eye: …but if they are an important enough part of my life they will eventually realize that that's how I have chosen to be

Under eye: They will realize that I have unshakable peace

Under nose: I will become know as a calm, serene person

Chin: I will attract serene thoughts and level-headed people to me

Collarbone: I know that I can choose serenity now and the Universe must gift me with things that match that which I have chosen

Under arm: My peaceful mind will help all of those around me achieve peace and serenity

Top of head: My relaxing and remaining serene is undoubtedly one of the best things that I can do for the world!

Chapter 18: I Am Ready to Receive my Soulmate now!

I demand my special partner now!

Eyebrow: In the past I have been too busy or introverted to find that special someone to share my life with

Side of eye: …it seemed like such a daunting task that I didn't want to face it

Under eye: …perhaps I thought that the right person would just fall into my lap at some point

Under nose: …perhaps I even feared that a new person in my life would take up too much of my time or energy

Chin: But now I know that the right person will give me energy and encourage me to get more done in less time!

Collarbone: I am ready, willing and able to have my special love now!

Under arm: I'm excited to see how the Universe will help deliver my future partner to me

Top of head: I'm excited to see what my new friend and partner is like!

Eyebrow: I'm going to push some of my relatively unimportant things off to the side and make room for my new romantic partner

Side of eye: I'll clean up my car a little and use feng shui to make my home more open and inviting

Under eye: I've been operating alone for long enough

Under nose: I'm ready to share my life with a wonderful person who adores me

Chin: I'm going to go to where I think I will meet my new love

Collarbone: I'm going to chat with interesting individuals until I find someone who makes my heart flutter!

Under arm: …and find a clever way to insert that person into my future

Top of head: Ha ha! I am so going to find someone new to love! WOOOOO!

Chapter 19: Moving closer to Joy and Myself by Identifying and pursuing my Life's Purpose(s)

This routine requires you to do a little work. You need to fill in the blanks spaces with your own personal story!

Eyebrow: In the past I have had a nagging feeling that I'm not living my life to the fullest

Side of eye: ...I felt as though there is a purpose that I hadn't fulfilled yet

Under eye: I didn't want to put time and effort into something before I even knew for certain that it was my life purpose

Under nose: If I knew my life purpose I would be inspired to take action to accomplish it!

Chin: I was happiest back when I was _____ because I was _____ and _____.

Collarbone: The times I felt most alive were when I _____ and _____.

Under arm: The right things for me are the things that delight me and bring me closer to me

Top of head: My life purpose will give me more freedom, lightness, expansion, awareness and joy

Eyebrow: I'm going to run towards things that excite me!

Side of eye: The best thing I can do is take the right action, the next best thing I can do is to take the wrong action and learn from my mistake

Under eye: The worst thing I can do is nothing

Under nose: I'm not going to waste my life in doubts and fears

Chin: I will have faith that the thing that calls to me now is the "work" that will open previously unseen doors to me and best prepare me for the future

Collarbone: The keys to my purpose-driven life are meaning and involvement

Under arm: All good people will help me achieve my goals and the Universe is offering me support and abundance if I simply agree to receive it

Top of head: Pursuing my purpose can be as simple as keeping my personal priorities in the forefront of my mind and trusting myself enough to consistently take action on my knowing

Chapter 20: I attract as many Lovers as I wish to have

This routine is for mature readers only!

I'm a Sexy person

Eyebrow: In the past I have been either too busy or too introverted to go out and get a lover

Side of eye: ...I either didn't put enough energy into it or just day-dreamed about it

Under eye: Now I'm ready to take action!

Under nose: I'm ready to go out and get a lover for myself!

Chin: My body deserves it

Collarbone: I deserve it

Under arm: I'm going to gift myself with someone who is seeking a fun partner like me

Top of head: Wow, now that I'm in this energy, like-minded people will be able to feel my sexuality!

Eyebrow: I'm going to go to where I think my future lover is

Side of eye: I'm not going to chicken out, instead I'm going to get close enough to a potential future lover to feel if their energy is right

Under eye: If I feel the right energy from them I'm going to initiate a conversation and see if they're the lucky one!

Under nose: If they aren't ready to accept my energy I will simply move on to the next person that I'm attracted to

Chin: When I find the right person I will take my new toy to a bedroom and make their toes curl!

Collarbone: I can keep my new lover as long as I want to

Under arm: When I am vibrating at the energetic frequency of sex other people in that energy will sense it and offer themselves to me

Top of head: I will have a delightful lover whenever I want one!

Chapter 21: Your Customizable Template

No one knows you as well as you know yourself, so who better to design your tapping routine than you?! With a little effort on your part you can put together the exact words that will help you break through anything you perceive to be limiting you. All you have to do is pick a topic and insert the appropriate phrases into the framework below...

Eyebrow: In the past I have believed that _____ [the belief you wish to change]

Side of eye: As a result of this I have _____ [identify what price you have paid for having this belief]

Under eye: I have also _____ [identify another negative thing that that limiting belief has created]

Under nose: I forgive myself for having had this belief

Chin: I am ready to move on!

Collarbone: I am ready to embrace a new, empowering belief

Under arm: My new belief will enable me to _____ [identify a benefit having your new, empowered belief will give you]

Top of head: From now on I will be known as _____ [the type of person who embodies the spirit of your new belief]

Eyebrow: I'm done being _____ [describe the type of person you choose not to be any longer]

Side of eye: I'm going to be the type of person who _____ [describe how a person fully embodying your new belief would be]

Under eye: I am going to _____ [your new empowered action] because it brings me closer to what I want

Under nose: I am going to _____ [your new empowered action] because it brings me closer to ME and I deserve it!

Chin: I will enjoy being _____ [your new empowered self] because it will allow me to _____ [identify how truly embodying your new belief will make your life easier and more joyful]

Collarbone: _____ [your term for "The Universe"] and all the millions and millions of good people in the world support me and want me to succeed

Under arm: I FEEL _____ [the quality of your new belief in your body] already and I will take the time to invite this feeling into my body on a daily basis

Top of head: _____ [your term for "The Universe"] only gives me ideas that I can use. If I can conceive it I can achieve it!

I certainly hope that you have fun doing the routines and they help make your life better in many ways! Peace, love, health, and outright joy to you!

Photography Credit: Claus Rebler

This book is for informational purposes only. The statements made in this book have not been evaluated by the FDA and are not intended to diagnose, treat, cure or prevent any disease. Anyone suffering with any medical or psychiatric condition should consult with a qualified medical professional to correctly identify the causes. © Copyright 2012, 2013 *Natural Cure Network, Inc.*

Printed in Great Britain
by Amazon.co.uk, Ltd.,
Marston Gate.